Original title:
Grapes of Summer

Copyright © 2025 Creative Arts Management OÜ
All rights reserved.

Author: Riley Donovan
ISBN HARDBACK: 978-1-80586-292-5
ISBN PAPERBACK: 978-1-80586-764-7

Juices of Joy

Plump little orbs, a feast for the eyes,
They bounce and they giggle, oh what a surprise!
With laughter they squirt, a messy delight,
On sunny warm days, they dance in the light.

Splashing on shirts, their colors so bold,
Sticky sweet stories, always retold.
In baskets they tumble, an orchestra's sound,
With each little burst, joy's lost can be found.

The Taste of Warmth

Sipping the sunshine, with flavors so bright,
Every drop smiles back, in this wild summer light.
Mouthfuls of honey, all wrapped in a swirl,
Each taste a delight, like a happy little twirl.

Cheeky little pests join in for the snack,
The ants throw a party, just to come back.
Sticky-fingered fun, oh what a grand feast,
Always a delight, never diminished, at least!

Grapevine Secrets

Whispering tales from the vine to the breeze,
The secrets of summers, spoken with ease.
Ripe are the stories, sweet and so sly,
They giggle with joy, as they mingle and pry.

"Oh look at that bunch, it's tragically spent!"
"What gossip do you hold, with your juicy content?"
They chuckle and chuck, like a group of jesters,
Turning each nibble to tales of the besters.

Blossom and Berry

In gardens they frolic, on branches they sway,
With laughter and cheer, they enjoy the ballet.
Chasing the bees, oh what a sight,
They tickle and tease, from morning till night.

Floating along, on a soft summer breeze,
With all their sweet charm, they aim to please.
Each pluck and each swirl, a burst of delight,
In the dance of the season, everything feels right.

Reflections in Green

In a field where laughter grows,
Sunshine tickles tiny toes.
Bunches dangle, oh so round,
Dance beneath the joy they found.

Wobbly legs and tipsy nights,
Bubbles pop and silly sights.
Chasing shadows, we all roam,
Stumbling home, we find our throne.

Twining Tendrils

Tendrils twist in playful ease,
Twirling round like summer breeze.
With a wink and cheeky grin,
They coax the sun to let us in.

Laughter spills like juice so sweet,
Sticky fingers, summer heat.
We'll sip our drinks and puff our chests,
And crown ourselves as summer's guests.

Golden Clusters Beneath the Sun

Clusters gleam with golden light,
Like dancers dressed for summer night.
Snagging snacks from every vine,
We nibble out our grand design.

With giggles loud and hats askew,
We toast to joys both tried and true.
Each sip and snack, a wild affair—
Watch out! That face is quite unfair!

The Lure of Vineyard Paths

Vineyard paths where mischief lies,
Underneath the azure skies.
Tip-toeing past the plump delight,
We rush for bites, oh what a sight!

Beneath the trees, we tell our tales,
With every sip, our laughter sails.
Summer's fling, we can't resist,
For in this fun, we coexist.

Warmth in Every Sip

In the glass, sunshine glows,
Tongue dances, joy overflowed.
Each sip a secret, sweet delight,
Chasing worries, taking flight.

Bold flavors tease, they play a game,
With every toast, they stake their claim.
Laughter bubbles, friends unite,
In this warmth, all feels right.

Curious Clusters

Bouncing bunches, such a sight,
Hiding mischief in the light.
'What's your secret?' one did ask,
'Just a laugh behind this mask!'

Round and jolly, sipping cheer,
Crafting giggles, no room for fear.
Clusters chatter under trees,
Telling stories with the breeze.

The Nectar Chronicles

Tales of sweetness, bold and bright,
Whispers of joy, in the night.
Each drop a giggle, every sip a cheer,
Chronicling laughs we hold so dear.

In this elixir, tales unfold,
Of clumsy dances and secrets told.
Mirth in every pour and spill,
A tapestry of laughter, we all feel.

Shadows Over the Orchard

Beneath the trees, giggles grow,
Shadows whisper secrets low.
'Do you see those shapes above?'
'Looks like grapes doing the cha-cha shove!'

Sunset paints a purple swirl,
Where fruit and laughter freely whirl.
In this orchard, joy is found,
As sunlight dips, we dance around.

A Rustic Elixir

In the sun, we squeeze a bunch,
Laughing as we fill our punch.
Sticky hands and purple stains,
We sip like kings, ignoring pains.

Barrels roll like clumsy sheep,
The neighbors side-eye, barely sleep.
We dance around in fruity jest,
Our laughter echoing, no time for rest.

Echoes in the Canopy

Beneath the trees, we find a snack,
Swinging from branches, never lack.
A squirrel steals our juicy prize,
We mock his speed and tiny size.

With every bite, our giggles burst,
Too much sun? Oh, we must quench thirst!
Yet straws keep bending, flying wide,
Our drinks are gone, our wits collide.

The Secret of the Soil

Digging deep, we struck a clue,
Worms are laughing, who knew, who knew?
They wiggle and dance with such delight,
While we just search for snacks so right.

The dirt was thick, the laughter loud,
We may have drawn quite a crowd.
The bounty's ripe, no one can see,
We've turned our toil into a spree.

Days of Abundance

Jars all lined, the colors bright,
We try to catch the summer light.
Fumbling lids and squishy jam,
We joke it's just a fruit to spam.

Friends arrive with smiley cheer,
"Mishaps happen, so bring your beer!"
With every spill and sticky plop,
Our laughter echoes, we'll never stop.

Sipping Sunlight

A glass of joy in hand we cheer,
With sunlight trapped, we hold it dear.
Sips of laughter, bubbles rise,
We toast to fun beneath the skies.

In shades of green, we linger long,
Wobbling dance to nature's song.
Fleeting moments, forget the grind,
With fruity smiles, we unwind.

Each sip a giggle, joy's embrace,
Plump little orbs, a sweet embrace.
The world spins round, our worries fade,
In this bright glass, our fears betrayed.

Chasing shadows, laughing loud,
In this warm glow, we feel so proud.
Hearts are light, spirits high,
As we sip sunshine, oh my, oh my!

Days of Fermented Bliss

Oh, the joy of vine-turned-gold,
The tales of summer thus retold.
In barrels deep, with patience stored,
The nectar flows, life we adored.

Sipping slowly, a quirky grin,
As honest fables chase the din.
With each pour, the tension fades,
Just silly dreams in glass cascades.

Uncork the laughter, let it roam,
In fizzy tales, we find our home.
Each fizzy pop brings fits of glee,
In this fermented jubilee.

We dance, we laugh, let worries drift,
As summers gifts ignite our shift.
With giggles clinking, we persist,
In fermented days, all fears dismissed!

Beneath the Arched Vines

Underneath the leafy trails,
We share our dreams and silly tales.
With every squish, a chuckle sounds,
As grape-like giggles bounce around.

Shady spots and playful jests,
In nature's hands, we find our rests.
Mosquitoes buzz, but we don't sweat,
Our laughter wafts, let's not forget.

We prance and frolic, toes a-squat,
In wiggle-pod experiments we caught.
Tickled pink by nature's muse,
In this wild world, we'll never lose.

The sun dips low, the evening calls,
With tipsy dreams behind the walls.
In every squabble and every dance,
Beneath the arches, we take a chance!

Nature's Palate

A platter bright, a feast of cheer,
With laughter ripe, let's commandeer.
Drizzles of chaos swirl with glee,
In nature's kitchen, wild and free.

From fruity frolics, flavors blend,
With cheeky bites that never end.
Tickled tongues on this grand spree,
As gusts of whimsy captivate thee.

Cheese and sun in perfect pair,
Round we giggle in this fresh air.
Each morsel sings, a joyful tune,
With mischief served beneath the moon.

So grab your forks, embrace the feast,
With nature's palette, joy increased.
As laughter spills, and spirits rise,
Banish the blues and claim the skies!

The Flavor of Warmth

The sun shines bright, a bold display,
Bouncing along the sunny way.
Bunches hang like tiny balls,
Underneath the leafy stalls.

Sipping juice of pure delight,
Spilling laughter, feeling light.
A sticky hand, a friendly fight,
Tasting magic, just right.

Backyard picnics, flavors blend,
With jokes that never seem to end.
Juicy squishes, giggles start,
Nature's candy warms the heart.

Vineyards and Vespers

In vineyards where the laughter grows,
Wobbly feet and quite the show.
Chasing squirrels and timid mice,
King of clumsy, rolling dice.

Tunes of evening fill the air,
Dinner tables, quite the flair.
Sips and bites, a merry song,
Who knew mishaps could feel so strong?

With tattered hats and shoes askew,
Friends all gather, just a few.
Under stars, the banter flows,
Old tales shared, and where time goes.

Essence of the Earth

The globe spins in vibrant glee,
Tiny orbs beneath the tree.
Sticky fingers trying to climb,
In the patch of pardonable crime.

Roaming spiders, cheeky thrills,
Swinging through the fragrant hills.
With splashes of laughter infused,
Who knew nature could be so amused?

Shadows dance on grassy beds,
While sticky treats fill all the heads.
Anointed by the evening gold,
Giggle fits never get old.

Sweetness Found

Beneath the sun, a playful chase,
Around the vines, a cheeky race.
Flavor bursts, a fruity tease,
Tummies rumble, "more, please, please!"

Rolling on the dewy grass,
The humor shared, the moments pass.
With jokes and jads, so light and free,
Sealed in laughter, joy's decree.

In every sip, a spark of cheer,
Nature's jest, forever near.
Life's a feast, come take a bite,
In silly dreams, we feel so bright.

Savoring Solstice

Beneath the sun, we stomp and dance,
With squished fruits, we take a chance.
Foot's the hero—what a treat!
Grape juice showers, sticky feet!

The neighbors glare, they think we're mad,
But oh, the laughter, oh so glad!
With every slip, a joyful cheer,
Just don't ask me to volunteer!

We pop the corks like summer fizz,
The fruity feast is all a whiz!
Each glass a toast, we giggle wide,
With fruit mustaches, we take pride!

When twilight falls, our voices blend,
The silly stories never end.
With every sip, the truth unwinds,
We toast to life and silliest finds!

From Blossom to Bottle

What's that smell? Oh, can you guess?
The vineyard's life is quite a mess!
Bumbles buzzing, laughter sings,
As clumsy lovers trip on strings!

The blossoms dance, they shimmy bright,
With tipsy bees that cause delight.
A caper here, a jiggle there,
Nature's soap opera in the air!

We gather fruit both plump and funny,
In sun-soaked glory, oh so runny!
With sticky hands, our harvest shines,
Then comes the corks—oh silly vines!

From countertop to frosty glass,
Our homemade brew just can't be classed.
It bubbles up, a fizzy roar,
Who knew mishaps could taste so poor?

A Summer's Banquet

A picnic spread in the warm sun's glance,
With treasures hidden in our prance.
Fruits all jumbled, salads wild,
Each bold flavor just makes us smile!

Tomatoes giggle, cucumbers play,
As pickles hum a song today.
The bread rolls rattle, what a scene,
If only plates could talk, they'd glean!

Desserts parade like fancy troops,
While we bob our heads in silly loops.
The pie's a triumph, the cake's a jest,
Onward we feast, it's for the best!

And when the day gives way to night,
Our food comas lead to silly fright.
With tummy aches, we play the game,
Who ate the most? They're never the same!

Twisted Vines and Tales

In twisted rows, the stories weave,
Of grapes that laugh and giggle, believe!
The drunken elves sing songs of cheer,
To vines that gossip, loud and clear!

The sun dips low, the shadows crawl,
As vintners dance and heed the call.
A barrel rolls, oh what a sight!
With every thump, our hearts take flight!

The moon creeps in, it starts to tease,
Whispers swirl like autumn leaves.
With every sip, we tell our fables,
Of friendship, wine, and laughter tables!

So raise a glass to all things odd,
In liquid gold, we find our god.
Who knew a vine could spark such glee,
In this wild world, just let it be!

Clusters of Joy

In the orchard, laughter grows,
With every pluck, a silly pose,
Juicy globes in every hand,
Sticky fingers, oh so grand.

A little pout, a playful frown,
Tumbling down, we roll around,
Chasing tails and sweet delight,
Bumbling bees join in the flight.

Squished and squashed, a berry fight,
We end the day with sheer delight,
Silly hats made from the vine,
Laughter echoes, spirits shine.

Soon we'll feast on juicy cheer,
With frosty drinks and friends so near,
Clusters of joy in every bite,
Making memories, pure and bright.

Sun-soaked Symphonies

Under the sun, we sing and sway,
Frolicking in the warmth of day,
A pinch of mischief in the air,
As juicy fruits lay everywhere.

With tickled toes and silly grins,
Rolling laughter as the fun begins,
Nature's tunes, a merry sound,
Shuffling feet on grassy ground.

The caterpillars join the dance,
Wiggly worms in a funny stance,
As butterflies float gracefully,
We join their flight, so blissfully.

Sunshine sprinkles all around,
In this silly, vibrant playground,
With every squeeze of ripened flesh,
We savor joy, we feel refreshed.

The Dance of Leaves

Leaves are twirling in a spree,
Like dancers wild, so carefree,
With each gust, they spin and twist,
Join the fun, you can't resist!

Underneath the shade so fine,
We sway and giggle, feeling divine,
A gust of wind, oh what a game,
As nature calls and plays its fame.

Watch out for the squirrels that tease,
As they scurry and shimmy with ease,
Dropping acorns, oh what a sight,
While we laugh with sheer delight.

In this leafy, lively show,
We dance and prance in bright sunlight glow,
Nature's joy wrapped in green and gold,
A playful tale that never gets old.

A Golden Harvest

With baskets brimming, off we go,
A treasure hunt through fields aglow,
Golden orbs hang from their vines,
Chasing giggles, crossing lines.

Sweaty brows and muddy shoes,
Tripping over, singing blues,
Each sweet bite's a wild surprise,
Sticky faces, laughing eyes.

The sun sets low, a brilliant hue,
We toast with juice, a fruity brew,
And for dessert, let's not forget,
More silly snacks without regret.

As evening falls, we share a cheer,
For all the joy we found right here,
With every nibble, laughter sparks,
In our hearts, the summer marks.

Fruitful Whispers

In the garden, laughter reigns,
Bouncing fruit on silly chains.
Berries giggle, apples roll,
Oranges dance, they've lost control.

Vines tangle like old friends do,
Hilarity in every hue.
Nectar drips like cheeky jokes,
Cowboy pears and silly yolks.

Sunshine beams on topsy-turvy,
Mangoes wearing hats, oh so swervy.
Pineapple wigs, all snazzy and bright,
What a sight, oh what a sight!

Gather round for the fruit parade,
Joking lemons in bright charade.
Watermelon slices so grand,
Their punchlines juicy, unplanned!

The Essence of Verdance

In the shade, a fruit feast starts,
Fruity giggles steal our hearts.
Cherries twirl, plum plays the flute,
Melons in hats, how they salute!

Grapefruit whispers, 'Pick me, now!'
Laughing loudly, I take a bow.
Peaches tease with fuzzy flair,
'Join our party, if you dare!'

Apples joke, 'We're the best!
Take a bite, it's a fruity test!'
Bananas slip and slide away,
In a game of chase, they play.

Berry jam becomes a tune,
Causing dance moves, oh so soon.
With each laugh, more fruit appears,
Sweet silliness for all our cheers!

Morning Dew on Leaves

Morning dew, a sneaky prank,
Kisses leaves like little tanks.
The sun peeks in with a hearty grin,
Droplets giggle, let the fun begin.

Cherries cluster, raucous chat,
As the squirrel plays, 'Where's my hat?'
With a twirl, the dew drops sway,
Nature's disco, come what may.

Beans in pods share silly tales,
Pumpkins tell of fishy gales.
Sunflowers bow with a sway so grand,
As if to say, 'Join our band!'

All the fruits bask in the glow,
Lemonade rivers begin to flow.
With each giggle, the day takes flight,
Morning's mischief feels just right!

Sunlit Journeys

Under the sun, a fruity quest,
Bananas boast, 'We're the best!'
Peaches prance on a sunny road,
Joking grapes all share the load.

Exotic fruits bring tales so wild,
Coconuts giggle, feeling like a child.
Watermelons roll with such delight,
In this silly, fruity fight.

Kiwi whispers, 'Let's be brave!
Join the fun or you won't save!'
Berry boats sail on juicy streams,
Gather 'round for fruity dreams.

Sunset chuckles, it's winding down,
As fruits parade through the town.
With laughter sweet and spirits high,
An orchard's joy beneath the sky!

Twilight Picking

Under the sky, we roam and giggle,
Bending low, we pluck and wiggle.
In the twilight's gentle glow,
Squeezing fruit, what a show!

A squished one here, a squished one there,
Juices running everywhere.
Laughter echoes through the night,
As fruit flies take their flight!

Our fingers stained, a silly sight,
Sticky laughs 'til dawn's first light.
Don't eat them all, save one or two,
For tomorrow, we'll still chew!

Embrace of the Sun

The sun is bright, the day's so fine,
Chasing shadows, sipping wine.
A feast of colors, sweet and bold,
The warmth of summer, young and old.

As we dance, the juice does spill,
Who knew that summer could fulfill?
Stomping grapes, a silly game,
Making juice, not seeking fame!

A splash of red, a dash of green,
Fruity chaos, quite the scene.
"Did you see that?" laughter flies,
As we toast to our sweet surprise!

Echoes of Summer's Fruits

Whispers of fruit in the warm breeze sing,
As we gather round, oh the joy they bring.
Picking and plopping, who knows the score?
One for you, and two for the floor!

"Oops!" giggles erupt, no one to see,
As a stranger than life bumblebee.
Buzzing by with a cheeky grin,
Stealing our snacks, what a win!

With every slip, there's laughter shared,
Splatters of juice as memories paired.
Who knew fruit could bring such glee?
In every bite, silly jubilee!

Vines in the Twilight

As shadows grow, we sway to cheer,
Among the vines, nothing to fear.
With every pluck, a grinning face,
Who knew fruit could make such a race?

"Catch that one!" a friend yells loud,
As we tumble, lost in the crowd.
A berry flies, an acrobatic feat,
Dodging juice, oh what a treat!

Lay back, relax, let worries flee,
Nature's bounty, wild and free.
Giggling fits by the soft moon's light,
Such silly fun in the warm twilight!

Sunlit Serenity

In fields where sunshine plays,
The fruits dangle, a hilarious maze.
Wobbling squirrels chase their dream,
While bees hum a buzz-worthy theme.

The farmer laughs, a hat so wide,
Chasing away goats with pride.
Rolling barrels, a slippery quest,
Dancing with grapes, oh what a jest!

The Art of Fermentation

Yeast in the air, oh what a smell,
Bubbles join in a fizzy spell.
Vines twist like a comic strip,
As laughter spills from every sip.

In barrels around, jokesters convene,
Pranking the grapes, oh so serene!
Tasting notes that tickle the tongue,
A symphony of fun, forever young.

A Toast to Nature

Raise a glass, let stories flow,
Of crows that sneak and rabbits that go.
A toast to the vines, so spry and bold,
With tales of mischief, joy to unfold.

Nature's banquet, a wild affair,
Mice in tuxedos, quite debonair.
Each sip a giggle, oh what delight,
As owls hoot in the moonlit night.

The Palette of the Vineyard

Colors burst in a playful scene,
Purple, green, a painter's dream.
Cheeky raccoons joining the fun,
Diving in buckets, oh what a run!

Splashes of laughter on every vine,
Nature's art, superbly divine.
So grab a brush, paint the day bright,
With every sip, the world feels right.

Bubbles in the Breeze

Tiny orbs float by with grace,
Catching sunlight's warm embrace.
Each one holds a giggle tight,
Bursting forth with pure delight.

Laughter leaps from every sip,
As bubbles dance in joyful trip.
Swirls of fizz and silly cheer,
Tip your glass, let's toast right here!

In meadow's warmth, carefree we play,
Chasing bubbles that drift away.
With every pop, a jest we share,
Life is sparkly, light as air!

So let's indulge in laughter's rays,
With bubbles leading us in praise.
Here's to silliness under the sun,
Where giggles and bubbles never shun!

Picnic Beneath the Boughs

A sprawling quilt upon the ground,
With tasty treats all piled round.
Sandwiches stacked with silly names,
And bets on who will win at games.

Ants march in a grand parade,
Stealing crumbs as if they've made,
A five-star meal to share and boast,
While we toast to the picnic host!

Sips of juice that dribble down,
Sticky fingers, laughter's crown.
We compete to see who's the messiest,
In this feast, we are the bestiest!

As sunlight dapples through the trees,
We munch and giggle, feeling ease.
A picnic legend we shall weave,
With memories we'll never leave!

When Sun Meets Soil

Golden rays touch the ground,
Whispered secrets all around.
Veggies wiggle, trying to peek,
'Oh look, here comes a garden sneak!'

With playful roots and tipsy vines,
Carrots dance and spin in lines.
Onions chuckle, while beets groove,
Sunshine kisses with every move.

Worms are squirming, wearing shades,
In this patch, pure joy parades.
Photosynthesis, the day's big show,
As petals ripple in a flow.

Joyful colors burst on sight,
Nature's joke, a pure delight.
With soil and sun in perfect bliss,
Let's laugh and dance, we can't resist!

Ripening Rhythms

Fruits are jiving on the vine,
Bouncing happy in a line.
Oranges twirl, apples sway,
It's a fruity cabaret!

Lemon slices burst with zest,
In this dance, they are the best.
Bananas peel back laughs galore,
As they tango across the floor!

Berries giggle, holding tight,
Ripe for fun, they're out of sight.
With every bump along the way,
We're fruit dancers, hip-hip-hooray!

So gather round and join the cheer,
In this orchard, there's nothing to fear.
As sweetness flows with every beat,
Let's ripen rhythms, feel the heat!

Nature's Wine

The plump ones dangle from the vine,
They whisper secrets, drink divine.
A splash of color, a bright delight,
Bottled giggles in the sunlight.

With every squish, a bubble bursts,
A fruity joke, a summer thirst.
Taste buds dance like kids at play,
Laughter spills, come join the fray.

A sip of joy, the world's a cheer,
Watch the bees do the cha-cha here.
Nature's joke in every clink,
A toast, a laugh, a perfect wink.

Sipping laughter, clinking glass,
Who knew wine could be such sass?
Under skies that giggle bright,
We share the fun, from day to night.

Juicy Promises

In the basket, treasures shine,
Round and ripe, a fruity line.
Each one teases with a grin,
Promises of sweetness within.

Pick a bunch, they bounce and roll,
Squeezing joy is the ultimate goal.
With every taste, a chuckle found,
Juicy secrets that abound.

A fruit parade, they burst with glee,
Who knew fruit could be so free?
We giggle, sip, and share delight,
Juicy laughs, our thirst ignites.

In the orchard, fun takes flight,
Crafting mischief with each bite.
Nature's pranks come bottled tight,
And laughter wins this sunny fight.

Twilight in the Vineyard

The sun dips low, a wink so sly,
In the vineyard, shadows sigh.
Bottle rockets in the blue,
Cheers to skies that hug us too.

Critters dance in shadows deep,
Whispers of wine, secrets we keep.
A playful breeze, a chuckle here,
As twilight drapes its cloak of cheer.

Clusters sway, like a silly game,
Under the stars, we stake our claim.
Toasting tales of summer nights,
Where humor thrives and joy ignites.

Dreams are poured from every cork,
With every sip, the laughter sparks.
As night approaches, let's embrace,
The funny side of nature's grace.

The Savor of Sunshine

With every drop, a sunbeam caught,
On lips, a memory, joy's sweet thought.
Clusters grin from leafy beds,
Bees are buzzing, a dance of heads.

Nectar flows like jokes in air,
Tasting sunshine, nothing can compare.
Sipping smiles from glasses tall,
Nature's laughter, after all.

Funny faces from a fruity blend,
While summer days seem never to end.
Swirling flavors, sweetness sings,
Laughter drips from all the things.

In this glass, we find our cheer,
To raise a toast with friends so dear.
The savor lingers, sweet and bright,
A sunny smile in every bite.

Harvest Moon Serenade

Under the moon, the vines do sway,
With dreams of wine at the end of the day.
The critters gather for a dance so fine,
But watch your step, or you'll trip on a vine!

Each cluster hangs like a globby hat,
A feast awaits, but oh! Where's my cat?
She's taking selfies, posing so bright,
While I'm here lost in the harvest night.

The farmers sing in silly tones,
While squirrels steal snacks from our old cologne.
In barrels, we'll stomp, just laugh and play,
And hope the neighbors keep their dogs at bay!

So raise a glass, let's toast the night,
To all the fun that's out of sight.
With tipsy giggles and wobbly cheer,
We'll sip on sunshine, for another year!

A Vineyard's Whisper

In a field where the vines twist and twine,
The bugs are buzzing, sipping honey wine.
A rabbit hops with a cheeky grin,
While we're just trying to keep the bugs in a bin.

The grapes are green, not quite ripe,
Like jokes we tell, they're sometimes tipe.
The farmer trips over shoes of his own,
And laughs out loud in a jovial tone.

Birds perch high, they croon like stars,
As we stomp on grapes and giggle from afar.
"Let's make a mess!" one shout did start,
And soon enough, we're all playing a part!

So here's to the munch, the crunch, and the fun,
In this crazy place where mischief's begun.
With tiny feet and giggles like bells,
We'll roast our stories and laugh till it swells.

Bunches Beneath the Sky

Beneath the sky, the clusters gleam,
With whispers of juice and a playful dream.
An ant in a tux brings a side dish of pie,
While the sun just laughs, guessing why we all try.

The breezes carry tales of cheer,
As we dodge the splashes of neighborly beer.
A grape juice fountain? What a surprise!
Warning: it splatters and stains with sweet lies!

The leaf hats dance to a silly tune,
As rabbits break out in a soft afternoon.
"A toast!" we shout with cups full of glee,
While dodging the flies doing a jig just for free!

So come along, let's prance as we toast,
To the bunches that make merry, we celebrate most.
With laughter a-plenty until we all fall,
For nothing feels better than sharing this all!

Summer's Liquid Treasure

The sun spills gold as we become bold,
To gather the laughter instead of the cold.
With barrels around and stories galore,
We sip on the nectar till we roar!

A splash of mischief in every glass,
Yeah, wine on our shirts? Oh, that's quite the class!
When grapes decide to go for a swim,
We're left with giggles and a chance to grin.

With sticky fingers and a wink in the air,
We toast to moments that none can compare.
"Oh, look at that!" someone shouts with glee,
As squishy snacks roll and flee from the spree!

So raise a cup, let's dance around,
With laughter escaping, we're joyfully bound.
Cheers to the chaos, the fun we bequeath,
And summer's sweet treasure that leaves us all beneath!

A Celebration of Flora

In the garden where giggles bloom,
Bees in bow ties dance and zoom.
Petunias wear polka dot hats,
While daisies flirt with sneaky cats.

Frolicking on a Sunday spree,
A squirrel steals fruit like it's free.
Sunflowers chuckle in the sun,
Chasing shadows just for fun.

Lettuce joins in with a squeal,
As carrots joke about their peel.
A radish rolls down a hill,
And everyone's laughing, what a thrill!

With every bloom, laughter grows,
A floral world where joy just glows.
Nature's jester, colorful sights,
In this garden, humor ignites!

Harvest Harmonies

In the orchard, apples conspire,
To strut and sing of their desire.
Pears in tuxedos twirl around,
While cherries giggle, cheerful sound.

Dance, dance, the fruit parade!
Strawberries join, with flair displayed.
Lemons grinning, all dressed in zest,
They leap and sway, oh what a fest!

Even plums are part of the show,
Making up jokes, stealing the glow.
Cucumbers chuckle from the vine,
"Who knew being crunchy could be so fine?"

Nature's humor fills the air,
As crops collide with funny flair.
In every laugh, there's sweetness found,
Harvest time, with joy abound!

Nature's Sweet Gift

Beneath the sun, the laughter grows,
As strawberries tell secrets in rows.
Melons pop jokes, tickling peas,
As they sway lightly with the breeze.

Each berry winks, a playful sprite,
Raspberries rave, with sheer delight.
Grapefruits giggle, not a care,
In this fruity fest, smiles to share.

Carrots compete in a funny race,
Hopping around, but lose their place!
As veggies chuckle, nature's grin,
Creating fun, where joy begins.

In every patch, a tale's well spun,
Nature's gifts bring laughter and fun.
A bounty of laughter, all aglow,
The sweetest treasures that we know!

The Romance of Ripeness

A watermelon winks from the vine,
While cantaloupe talks about fine wine.
Berries blush in the rosy light,
As they flirt with each other, what a sight!

The peach and the plum dance close and tight,
Spinning around under the moonlight.
A love story told in the orchard's embrace,
Where every fruit finds its place.

Bananas serenade with a twisty song,
As pears debate on what's right or wrong.
"Let's ripen together!" they call with glee,
In this orchard of love, just wait and see.

With every nibble, sweet tales unfold,
The romance of ripeness, a delight to behold.
Join the laughter, let joy take flight,
Where fruits fall in love, under shimmering light!

Lush Canopies and Laughter

Under green canopies we meet,
The sun plays hide and seek.
With sticky fingers, we munch and chew,
The fruit makes everything feel brand new.

Bouncing from branch to branch,
Like squirrels in a fruity dance.
A joke here, a laugh there,
We're all too full, no one seems to care.

Juicy squirts and giggles loud,
We frolic, feeling oh so proud.
Each bite is a burst, oh what a thrill,
Who knew a snack could give such a chill?

Chasing shadows, chasing fun,
Who knew eating could be so run?
With every swing and every grin,
We find the joy that lies within.

Nectar in the Breeze

Sweet whispers float on the air,
Like bees caught in a comical snare.
Bumblebees buzz with a silly sport,
Gathering goodness for their sweet sort.

Sticky fingers and messy faces,
We giggle and tumble in sunny spaces.
A splash of juice upon the lawn,
We laugh and shout, 'Just carry on!'

Chasing bubbles that float like dreams,
Nature's laughter bursting at the seams.
We trip and tumble, in sticky delight,
Who knew snacks could bring such a sight?

A race through vines, we hop and skip,
Grinning wide on our juicy trip.
The day drifts by in sweet refrain,
Who knew fun could come with such a stain?

Wine-Stained Dreams

In the vineyard, dreams collide,
As we sip on joy, our worries slide.
Purple stains on a shirt or two,
Oh dear, what else is new?

Dancing boots on sun-kissed ground,
Laughter echoes, joy is found.
A splash of juice, a giggling squish,
Wish I could always have this dish!

Discussing flavors, oh so bold,
Like tasting stories yet untold.
For every sip, a joke erupts,
We tumble through life, uninterrupt.

With friends by side, we toast our cheer,
"More fruit!" we cry, "let's persevere!"
Dreams of sweetness fill the air,
Join us now, no need to spare!

A Season's Bounty

Wander through the fields so bright,
Fruits falling like a funny sight.
With baskets full, we trip and sway,
Nature's bounty leads us astray!

We pluck and stash, a merry spree,
Sharing mishaps, laughing with glee.
With juice on our cheeks, we dance round,
Oh, what a season we have found!

Frolicking with a bounce in our step,
Jumping high, not one misstep!
Laden with laughter, treats galore,
We roll down hills, demanding more!

When dusk arrives, our hearts still sing,
What fun we had, what joy we bring!
With every fruity tale we tell,
A hearty laugh binds us all so well.

Whispers Among the Rows

In rows so neat, the fruit resides,
Shh, the sun is playing hide and seek.
A bunch in shades of green and blue,
They giggle softly, what a cheek!

A plump one said, 'I'm quite a catch,'
While hanging low, it lost a fight.
A hungry bird, with fancy match,
Declared it lunch, then took to flight.

The breeze comes in, a cheeky tease,
It rustles leaves, a playful dance.
With every sigh, they bend with ease,
Creating chaos in this prance.

So here we stand, amidst the fun,
A silly bunch, we're full of cheer.
In this parade beneath the sun,
We laugh, we roll, and share our beer.

The Palette of Summer

Oh look there's purple, orange, and green,
The fridge is stacked, bursting with glee.
I dare you to guess just what I mean,
    Sweet summer treats for all to see!

With every bite, a giggle escapes,
As juice runs down, it makes me grin.
The sticky hugs and funny shapes,
    A fruity situation we're in!

The blender roars like a lion fierce,
While sloshing juice makes quite the mess.
But all those splatters, they just pierce,
    The heart with joy – it's summer's best!

So raise your glass with fruity cheer,
    A toast to laughter in the sun.
With every sip, let out a cheer,
    For all the joy that's just begun!

Beneath Verdant Arches

Underneath these leafy shades,
We gather round for merry snacks.
The tails of whispers fill the glades,
As laughter echoes – what a knack!

The vines have secrets, tales to share,
Of summers past and fruit so grand.
A shocking truth – they can't compare,
To jelly stains upon my hand.

But where's the fun without a spill?
The neighbors peek, and giggle loud.
A table dance, an accidental thrill,
We're quite the messy, joyful crowd!

So gather 'round and join the jest,
Beneath these arches, life is sweet.
With every bite, we're truly blessed,
In vines of laughter, none can beat!

An Ode to the Vines

Oh, slender stalks, so full of charm,
You tickle noses when we pass.
With every twist, you raise alarm,
That summer's here – let's raise a glass!

Your leafy arms embrace the sun,
While teasing flavors dazzle loud.
A real-life game of hide and run,
Among your bounty, we're so proud!

From ferment dreams to fizzy fun,
What magical mischief do you weave?
In every juice, the laughter's spun,
With silly grins, we can't believe!

So here's to you, my lovely vines,
May summer bring you endless rays.
In every glass, your joy aligns,
Let's drink and laugh through sunny days!

A Symphony of Roots

In the garden they grow, so proud and stout,
With tender leaves waving, they laugh and shout.
They dream of the sun and dance in the breeze,
Hiding from squirrels and dodging the bees.

Some claim they're dancers, some say they're shy,
Whispering secrets as the days pass by.
With every plump bump, they tease and they jest,
Wondering who'll choose them, a date for the fest!

They boast of their sweetness, their tangy delight,
Telling tall tales in the cool autumn night.
Each one with a story, a laugh to unfold,
Of brave little bugs and the sun's bright gold.

So join in the chorus, the roots below sing,
Of folly and fun that the harvest will bring.
They band together, in joy, not in strife,
For summer's warm hug is the essence of life.

Memories in a Bottle

In a corked little jar, they chatter and cheer,
Recalling their journeys, from far and near.
They bounce with the bubbles, all jittery and bright,
Wishing for labels, to share their delight.

'Tell me your secrets!' a fizzy one calls,
'I'll tell you my dreams of the grand tasting halls!'
They giggle and swirl, as they spin on the shelf,
Only for curious folks, collecting themselves.

They love a good party, a toast or a bash,
Dancing and swirling, quite the bubbly splash!
Yet spill one little drop, what a humongous mess,
The floor turns into a sticky, sweet crest!

With every rewind of corks, cheers echo about,
In whispers they share, till the night's all but out.
Captured in glass, they eternally beam,
A toast to the laughter, a summertime dream!

Vines Under Starlight

Under the stars where the critters will play,
Vines giggle softly, in a dreamy ballet.
With moonbeams as spotlights, they twirl and they sway,
Frolicking freely till the break of the day.

They chat with the fireflies, sharing their tales,
Of comical hiccups and slippery trails.
With friends in the orchard, oh what a delight,
Racing with shadows, till the end of the night.

A raccoon named Morty will join in the fun,
Trying to steal bits of the ripened, round sun.
The vines say, 'Stop it!' in laughter, 'Not you!'
'You're far too cheeky for much more than a stew!'

So under the starlight, together they dream,
Of flavors and fables, of giggles and gleam.
With viney embrace, they revel in cheer,
For joy grows like wildflowers, all through the year.

Vineyard Reveries

In twilight's embrace, the vines weave their song,
Jesting and jiving, they've all gotten along.
They tickle the tendrils, as shadows start creep,
In a viny vineyard, where laughter runs deep.

Crazy adventures, a party so grand,
With a sprightly old beetle leading the band.
They sing of the rain and the sun's bright crown,
And how sipping on nectar never lets you down.

Amidst the green leaves, the grapes spin their tales,
Of clumsy green frogs and of wind-blown sails.
Each cluster a story, a giggle tucked tight,
Each vintage an echo of this pure delight.

So when you uncork, know it's laughter you stake,
In each cheerful sip, you'll remember the break.
For in every harvest, a pun waits to bloom,
A banquet of smiles sharing joy through the gloom.

A Tapestry of Green

In fields of emerald, laughter grows,
Nature's candies hang in rows.
With plump little spheres, the sun does beam,
Buzzing bees dance, plotting a scheme.

A picnic planned, the fruits are ripe,
But ants march in, they like the hype.
Who knew a feast would start a fight?
The flies all buzz, oh what a sight!

With each sweet bite, a giggle slips,
Juice drips down, a sticky grip.
We laugh at mess, it's pure delight,
Summer's hilarity, a joyful rite.

So here we sit, beneath a tree,
With silly hats and birds in spree.
Nature's platter, we can't resist,
In this green realm, we coexist.

The Bounty of Bloom

A basket full of round delights,
Tumbling giggles, playful sights.
With every taste, a silly face,
Like little moons, they dance in space.

Plucking fruit, what a grand chase,
Dodging wasps, oh what a race!
The juice flows free, we can't contain,
Our laughter rings, it's pure champagne.

With sticky fingers, we all cheer,
A feast of flavors, oh so dear.
But who knew the fruit could squirt?
Now my shirt's a messy dirt!

As friends unite, our hearts ignite,
Under the sun, we feel just right.
In nature's field, joy does loom,
Life's a comedy; let's assume!

To Taste the Golden Hours

In warmth of dusk, with smiles aglow,
We sip the sun; it steals the show.
Each moment sweet, a comic twist,
Trying to catch the drops we missed.

The crunch of laughter fills the air,
With each bold bite, we haven't a care.
A twist, a spin, and off they fly,
Like frisbees tossed to the sky!

Wobbly legs and giggly glee,
Running 'round like silly bees.
Fruits rolling 'round like little balls,
Hilarity echoes in nature's halls.

With every giggle, day bids adieu,
We toast together, a fun crew.
Chasing sunsets, our spirits rise,
Golden hours bring sweet surprise.

Autumn Kisses on Green

As autumn whispers to the leaves,
We joke about where nature weaves.
Each vine entwined in rich embrace,
Where giggles dance and joy finds space.

A snack parade, we storm the patch,
In search of fruit, the perfect match.
But sneaky squirrels plot to partake,
Leaving us laughing in their wake.

Their antics cause a joyful spree,
As nibbles vanish, we all agree.
Though autumn's chill begins to bite,
In fields of green, we feel just right.

With fruity chuckles all around,
We gather 'round, the joy is found.
A chorus of mirth, bright as can be,
In nature's play, we roam so free.

Lavender Skies and Luscious Harvests

Under lavender skies, we dance with glee,
Laughing with the bees, as wild as can be.
Chasing juicy thoughts, we munch on the fun,
While sticky fingers reach for the hot summer sun.

A bunch rolls away, it giggles with pride,
Wobbling like jelly, it knows how to glide.
We point and we chuckle at its silly spree,
Grapes on the loose, oh, what a sight to see!

With chairs turned upside down, we make a grand throne,

Sipping on sweet juices, we laugh and we moan.
The harvest is here, let's party till night,
Even squirrels join in, oh what a delight!

In a world filled with joy, we've cast out the gloom,
Wearing fruit hats, we dance in the room.
When laughter's the currency, we're all millionaires,
Under lavender skies, without worldly cares.

A Symphony of Ripeness

A symphony's playing, oh can you hear?
The plump voices call, so joyful and clear.
Instruments of flavor, so juicy and bright,
Each note is a burst, a taste of delight.

Clusters are jamming, a party they throw,
Swinging on vines, putting on quite the show.
With belly laughs echoing, the chorus takes flight,
Summer's sweet bounty, a jubilant sight!

Ripe fruit is singing, a satirical song,
With a few unexpected notes, they'll play all night long.
Every plop and every squish, a crescendo divine,
As we dance with the harvest, it's simply sublime!

When the trumpet's a watermelon, the fiddle a rind,
We laugh until we're crying, oh how sweetly unlined!
In the orchard's embrace, we'll frolic and sway,
A symphony of ripeness that won't fade away.

The Earth's Succulent Surrender

The earth gives a wink, with a smile oh so sly,
A bounty of fun, as season's clouds fly.
Juicy pockets brim with laughter and cheer,
A secret's revealed, summer's bounty is near.

Going on quests, looking under each leaf,
In pursuit of sweet bites, bring joy not grief.
With a skip and a hop, we pluck them with flair,
Tiny treasures bouncin', light as the air!

Fruits roll in circles, a merry parade,
Tickling our toes, their antics displayed.
A game of delight, we laugh and we shout,
In nature's own theater, there's never a drought!

With sticky fingers stained, we reminisce,
Every bite is a memory, one not to miss.
The earth's cheerful yield, a bounty so grand,
Golden laughter flows like the finest of brand.

Drifting into Autumn's Embrace

As summer waves bye, in a playful retreat,
We toss little morsels, it's time for a feast!
With smoothies and giggles, we float through the air,
While the sun whispers secrets, so light, so rare.

Ripe fruits rolling off, like marbles in play,
Cheeky and pesky, they stray on their way.
In the orchard we frolic, oh laughter explodes,
As vines link their arms, like jubilant roads!

Breezy afternoons, with sunshine as gold,
To every laughter, a story unfolds.
With whispers of autumn, a soft, silly shake,
We dance with the harvest, oh, what fun we make!

The fruits wink goodbye, their season now done,
But the laughter remains—oh, it's only begun.
Drifting through fall, with smiles still aglow,
In nature's embrace, our joy's set to grow!

Vineyard Whispers

In rows they stand, all plump and round,
Chattering softly, making a sound.
One said, 'Hey, can you feel the breeze?'
The other replied, 'Only if you please!'

They giggle and sway, a funny affair,
Debating if sunlight can grow their hair.
'You think we're all juice?' a bold one claimed,
'Just wait till the harvest; I won't be tamed!'

A squirrel passed by with a twitching tail,
They called out, 'Hey buddy, join our trail!'
He paused for a sec, then dashed away fast,
'Guess he can't handle our charming cast!'

With laughter and fun, they bask in the glow,
The sun keeps them happy from head to toe.
Just waiting for friends who love a good cheer,
These cheeky delights bring joy all year!

Harvest Moon Serenade

Under the moonlight, they start to dance,
Twisting and turning, they take a chance.
One grape slipped, said, 'I'm feeling quite bold!'
The others laughed, 'Come on, be sold!'

A shadow passed by, what could it be?
A raccoon with dreams of a late-night spree!
'Care to join in for a sweet little bite?'
'Only if you promise it won't be a fright!'

They share silly tales of days gone by,
Like the one who dreamed he could reach the sky.
'If only we had some wings to spread wide,'
They wheezed as they chuckled, heads side to side.

As night drapes gently over the field,
A symphony plays, the secrets revealed.
In joy they linger, till dawn makes its call,
These jolly round friends, the best of them all!

Sun-Kissed Bunches

Gather 'round, it's time to play,
Under the sun, we'll laugh away.
With our skins just a little bit tight,
We'll toast to the fun, from morning to night!

One said, 'I heard we're the star of the show!'
Another chimed in, 'Just don't steal the glow!'
So they danced under rays, so bold and bright,
Making each moment a sheer delight!

A ladybug joined, with a jig of her own,
They rolled with laughter, feeling right at home.
'Can you hear that tune? It's a grapevine beat!'
'Let's tango and twirl, move your little feet!'

With whispers of sweetness, the day grew long,
They sang all together, a fruity song.
Joyfully basking in sunshine's embrace,
These sun-kissed wonders, a jubilant race!

The Sweetness of Ripeness

In a leafy bowl, the sweetness begins,
Shimm'ring with laughter, where the fun never ends.
'Look at us now,' cries the plumpest of three,
'We're practically royalty—come taste and see!'

The wind took a whiff, and chuckled with glee,
'You've been hanging out quite stupidly!'
They giggled back, 'At least we are ripe!'
'But who knew grapes could be such a type?'

A bee zoomed by, with a curious buzz,
'What's all this fuss about sweetness and fuzz?'
'Join our parade, share joy and delight!'
And off they all went, till the fall of night.

With a plop and a giggle, they blended so fine,
Creating sweet tales, all cozy and vine.
Every drop with a story, a twist or a spin,
In the laughter of ripeness, let the fun begin!

Nectar of the Land

In a field where berries bounce,
The laughter rolls like a merry flounce.
Juice drips down from cheek to chin,
A playful race, let the feast begin!

Vineyards stretch, a playful maze,
With bunches hanging like green hoorays.
A cheeky bee buzzes with glee,
Hoping for drops that sweetly flee.

Sipping sunshine in every drop,
A clumsy sip makes the giggles pop.
From clusters bold to timid vines,
We toast to fun and silly signs!

So raise your glass, let joy expand,
In this merry world, we take our stand.
With every sip, a joke they say,
In laughter's vineyard, we'll always play!

The Orchard's Lullaby

Beneath the trees, a cozy nest,
Where squirrels nap and birds contest.
A drowsy sun sinks low and round,
While mulled-up dreams roll on the ground.

Swinging high on leafy swings,
The orchard hums of funny things.
A bee, a bloom, a bumblebee,
All tangoing in sweet esprit!

Foot races start for the plumpest plum,
Yet every runner trips on gum.
With sticky fingers and silly grins,
We laugh and cheer, our summer wins!

As night descends, the fireflies gleam,
Bright lights flicker in sleepy dream.
With whispers soft, the trees embrace,
Each giggle stitched in time and space!

A Tasting of Time

Sip the years like fine, bold wine,
With every gulp, let memories shine.
A clumsy cork pops, laughter spills,
As friends collide on rolling hills.

Each bottle hold a silly tale,
Of drunken bees and playful fails.
A splash of joy with a dash of cheer,
A taste of time etched crystal clear.

Oh, the laughter ages fine and sweet,
As grumpy old vines make friends discreet.
We sip and share, the stories flow,
In every bottle, giggles grow!

So raise your glasses, memories galore,
In life's great banquet, there's always more.
With every taste, the fun unwinds,
To savor moments, and leave behind!

Uncorking Memories

With a pop and a fizz, we break the seal,
Each cork released is a funny deal.
Giggles echo in the bubbling brew,
With every sip, there's more to pursue!

Oddly shaped glasses swirl with delight,
While spilled juice turns into a sight.
The table's a mess, but spirits are high,
As fruity flavors dance and sigh.

Old jokes tumble without much care,
Each punchline lands like a wild hair.
From puns about fruit to laughter's spree,
We weave our tales with glee and free.

So here's to the whims, the joy we find,
In bottles uncorked to ease the mind.
Each glancing toast, a memory's spark,
In our funny adventure, we leave a mark!

The Lush Green Tapestry

In the garden, plants do jig,
Dancing leaves, oh what a gig!
Bees are buzzing, buzzing loud,
Nature's joy, it draws a crowd.

Squirrels plotting on a spree,
Nibbling gems, they're quite the spree!
They wear tiny crowns of leaves,
Pretend royalty, as one believes.

Mice have joined the soirée fun,
With tiny hats, they're second to none!
The ground's a stage, the sun's the light,
Insects twirl till the fall of night.

A twist of fate, a vine's surprise,
Clowns in cabbages, oh how they rise!
Ripe with laughter, bursting bright,
Harvest fools in pure delight.

Fermented Dreams

Once a fruit, now drummists thump,
In barrels deep, they make a jump!
Bubble parties in their skin,
With every sip, let the fun begin!

Chubby cheeks and tipsy grins,
They toast to life, where laughter spins.
Squishy goodness, they roll and sway,
Bottled giggles brighten the day.

Spill the fun, oh what a scene,
Gurgling joy— a bubbly scream!
Dance of flavors, tickle the tongue,
In every drop, a song is sung.

Vines take flight, like silly kites,
In dreams of fizz, they soar to heights.
With frothy laughs, they greet the night,
In fermented dreams, all is right.

Sun-kissed Jewels

Beneath the sun, they gleam and shine,
Droplets of joy from the vine align.
With silly hats, the fruits parade,
In nature's circus, laughter's made.

Petals blushing with delight,
Winking at bugs, what a sight!
Squishing toes in oozing bliss,
A fruity dance, how could we miss?

Jewel-toned shades all around,
Fruitful hiccups on the ground.
With each plop, giggles arise,
Sun-kissed morsels, sweet surprise.

In the basket, a playful race,
Rolling fast with silly grace.
Fruits in laughter, joy in spree,
Sun-kissed gems, wild and free!

Ripened in the Warmth

Cuddled close, the leaves entwine,
Fruitful whispers, oh so fine!
Mirthy mimosas in the air,
Sharing secrets without a care.

Chasing shadows that tease the ground,
Frolicsome vibes all around.
With cheeky smiles, the sun takes aim,
In this warmth, all fruits proclaim.

Tickled pink by summer's breeze,
Bouncing to the laughter's tease.
Fruits play games, calling the shots,
A comedy where none are knots.

Bursting laughter, ripened cheer,
In the warmth, we persevere.
Joyful squabbles in the shade,
From this warmth, we won't evade.

www.ingramcontent.com/pod-product-compliance
Lightning Source LLC
Chambersburg PA
CBHW062108280426
43661CB00086B/340